FLASHBACK

FLASHBACK

V JEAN TYLER

Date of Publication: December 2002
Reprinted: August 2003

Published by:
Heronslake Hertz

Printed by:
ProPrint
Riverside Cottage
Great North Road
Stibbington
Peterborough PE8 6LR

ISBN: 0-6543822-0-X

CONTENTS

V   Repairs!

VI   Touch of Travel

VII   Nearer Home

VIII   Music

IX   Jubilee

INTRODUCTION

I have always scribbled poetry and prose for my own amusement and have fond memories of winning a competition in the Children's section of the Liverpool Echo entitled 'Going to School' over sixty years ago!

I was born and brought up in Liverpool where I attended the Medical School, and although I have lived in Devon for over forty years, I still have a great affection for that city and enjoy its poets.

My late husband was a veterinary surgeon and it is only since his death eleven years ago when I joined a local writers' group, that I have taken writing more seriously. Committing thoughts and anxieties to paper especially in times of crisis, has been quite cathartic and therapeutic: initially the emotions seem to settle more comfortably on the page than in conversation. In lighter vein, I find it easier to idly criticise or poke fun at colleagues or local situations in some rhyming nonsense than in stark spoken appraisal!

The opportunity to listen to others' work at 'First Thursday' the Torrington Writers' Group has added another dimension to my interest, and it was their sporadic approval which encouraged me to submit pieces which have appeared in Poetry now, Triumph House, Arrival Press and Anchor Books publications, and now to put together this collection.

I've started with 'Abiding Sheep' simply because I like this poem and I have a great personal affinity for ovines. I was so grateful to escape the cruel Foot and Mouth cull. The next section moves through sexual attraction, the joy of birth and family life with its occasional ecliptic passage, to the inevitable end which has its comforting aspects as well as its sorrow.

Thence there are a few observations on seasonal changes, the revitalising effect of spring, nature's response and the reassuring routine of the garden.

It is something of a salutary experience for a doctor to be an in-patient, and the necessary period of relative inactivity following my very successful hip replacement, gave me plenty of time for reflection and writing. Restored mobility meant I could satisfy my craving for travel every January.

The rest of the year I am usually involved in some amateur music and/or drama production. I love singing, especially lieder.

Finally I had to include HM The Queen in this her Jubilee year: well she is my generation and oh how the world has changed!

ACKNOWLEDGEMENTS

Thanks to ProPrint for their help and advice.

Special thanks to the 'First Thursday' writers' group Torrington
for their encouragement and for making writing
so enjoyable.

To dear John
The only love of my life

ABIDING SHEEP

A Devon Longwool octave makes my hobby flock
Arusha is the strongest of short-legged stubby stock
Plumped into a cushion by Afro-fashioned fleece
A teased-out curling staple springs back upon release.

Floreana is a gentle soul, a patchwork of a face
With features finely painted like a film of Breton lace
She's hesitant and timid as was her ovine mother
But when the ram arrived she made an ardent lover!

Isabella's very feminine, a Barbara Cartland frothy
She shelters ostentatiously inside the north field bothy
A carping high-pitched bleat brings the rest to gaze
But she's only calling 'ewe' again: they drift away and graze.

Serengetti born the year I went to Tanzania
Strides like an ancient leopard through the plains of yesteryear
She is calm and full of wisdom and leads the flock to feed
On last year's parsnips, stringy greens, with just a hint of greed.

Malvena, an adventurer, hedged through my Steptoe fence
To join the Cluns next door for greener grass and thence
Across the road where ivy draped a painted pale
Wolfed the powerful poison: here ends her deadly tale.

Belinda is a beauty, soft-fleeced, wide-eyed and cream
She tempts the Suffolk ram to boil a head of steam
The teasing in between time gives appassionato trouble
But on sunny Easter Sunday, she proudly drops a double.

Cecilia, Fiona and Fiesta; Devon Longwool ewes.   VJT

Sallylightfoot named after Darwin's islands' crab
Has a somewhat sideways gait and the gift of bleating gab
Her tone is quite melodious, a comfort in the dark
When the vixen weirdly calls for her partner's mating bark.

And finally there's Viney, a frumpy matron now
With heavy legs and limping, tousled wool and furrowed brow
But she's a well-tried lady slung low with her fourth lamb
With the confident control she attested with the ram.

There's a prevalent opinion here,
- and sometimes abroad
That sheep are dim and stupid,
Quite boring and quite bored
Someone might say of humans
'They're like a flock of sheep'
In my book that's a compliment
For sheep their counsel keep.

II   ARRIVAL, SURVIVAL AND DEPARTURE

SURVIVAL OF THE SPECIES

He came keenly at three with ostensibly a mission
To revise and teach her more about binary fission
She warmed to his subject, human biology
An essential ingredient for the June GCSE

They studied inflorescence of the plaintain and the thistle
The calyx and corolla, the carpels and the pistil
Then moved on to the earthworm and its adult reproduction
On the surface of the lawn, a nocturnal seduction

Thence to crawling crayfish which mate late in September
And cockroaches which turn their backs to make love and remember
They continued through the gamut of Darwin's evolution
The dogfish and the frog with its well-known spawn solution

And finally to mammals where they made a close connection
Understood so well the natural selection
They made love on a Sunday in the heat of afternoon
Both fresh and nubile virgins, he came a sperm too soon.

Years later tho' in harness with a splendid A N Other
She still knows deep nostalgia for her first, her student lover
A wormcast on the grass, a frogspawn distribution
Make her smile quietly for - Darwin's evolution.

DROP-IN, DROP-OUT

Eyes open wide
Like her legs I suspect
A pregnancy
Not hard to detect

Too late
For post-coital manoeuvre
Options - keep or succumb
To womb vacuum hoover

She shivers a trifle
Eyes staring still
Then shelters in laughter
A nervous high trill

'I'll go for adoption'
Her wide eyes now darting
Has she any idea
Of the grief of such parting?

The flesh of her flesh
Which she'll love without knowing
Will ache in her heart
When it comes to the going.

We talk of her mother
Alone - and her schooling
She's sure she will cope
Oh who is she fooling?

But: -
The decision is hers
Tho' she's only thirteen
No stark termination
For this coupling queen.

RETURNED, DAMAGED GOODS

She had him back
She loved him
What else could she do?
She'd played her part
Yet knew by heart
There'd be a déjà-vu.

She'd married him for love
For better or for worse
But then she'd no idea
Of his consuming curse

And now there were the children
Of both, not his or hers
She remembered how he'd
bathed them
And carried them upstairs
Then a cameo of comfort
A natural submission
But now she had the torture
Of a burrowing suspicion . . .

Was he abused?
How'd he become
This stranger in her bed?
The thought of 'the accused'
In court with full report
Filled her soul with dread.

The neighbours knew already
She sensed their quiet attack
'She must have known, oh surely'
And 'Why did she have him back?'

A few had shewn her kindness
In that once forgotten year
But now all was remembered
Dismembered, shame and fear.

Her mother wept
Her father kept
His counsel but his face
Showed deepest hurt
He held her
In the silence of embrace.

A LIFE INSIDE

How long was his life?
As long as we remember
Accomplished in the warm
Of a womb one soft September

First movements brought great joy
Enhanced anticipation
Then disturbed with super strength
A drowning desperation

He was born completely still
A stillbirth to the world
Body beautiful complete
A wisp of hair that curled

He saw none of the people
Very few saw him
And yet we hurt with loss
Grief flowing from the brim

In mind he'll live for ever
In the brightness of the dawn
A glowing evening sunset
A lamb just newly born

A swallow may fly early
Leave the milling flock
Mount a soaring thermal
Leave a life in hock

No one is ever lost
Intangible an essence
Lingers gently on
A comfortable presence

THE LONG JOURNEY

It took nine months, her passage
From beginning to the finish
It started unexpectedly -
Which in no way should diminish
The triumph of survival
Through the darkness on the way
And the ultimate emergence
Into the light of day.

The inception was quite small
You might say microscopic
She forged her path relentlessly
Static could mean ectopic
En route she found a cove
Fronded welcoming and warm
She wriggled in for comfort
Just before a violent storm.

Here she grew in stature
Fed gently by her host
Who would pat her at a distance
And smile a quiet boast
She thought she'd stay for ever
Tho she fancied larger quarters
Her limbs were folded up and in
Like some Darwinian tortoise.

She listened to the music
In the waters where she lay
And the voice of someone singing
'cross an ocean far away
These were tones of comfort
Of tenderness and love
And now and then seemed nearer-
Like a foot or two above!

Then exactly forty weeks
From the day of her creation
The walls around her cove caved in
With rhythm and gyration
She really couldn't linger -
She thought she might have drowned
The force drove her head first
This was no time to turn round.

She went onwards with the flow
Unhappy with the heat
The narrow route, the pressure -
Not something she'd repeat
Then it was over, she was free
There were people, quite a crowd
They all seemed much elated
(Did they have to talk so loud?)

One shouted 'It's a girl!'
Well, she'd known all along
Then again that tuneful drifting-
So this was mother's song
Out into the wide world
Solo, separate - (and adored)
But still plugged in, connected
By a more substantial chord

SUMMER BABY

I love you Isabella
Arousing protection
My tenth little special
Genetic connection

You're neat and compact
Hungry for life
A joyous relief
For my son and his wife

To hold you is bliss
For me such a wonder
Stirs me to tears
And also to ponder
How most babies come
Safely, intact
Yet this couple know
What it's like to be racked
By deep disappointment
Of George whom they lost
A salutary phase
An emotional cost

Today sees a new moon
In silver clear sky
Heralding summer
To raise spirits high

So welcome dear girl
To the spring of your days
My darling beginner
With love-winning ways.

MORTAL LINKS

A generation's outing, a brilliant day in March
Granny, elder daughter, daughter's daughter Lily Darch
They walk the quay at Hartland, spy a fulmar's nest
(Lily is just three years old and talks her very best).

They picnic in a field upon the family rug
And spread out all the goodies from the ancient family trug
Later they hike to Stoke, view the churchyard stones
And read historic glimpses of long-disjointed bones.

Mother's fingers trace the letters, wind-smoothed and lichen-green
Dispel the granite's fetters to read who may have been
Head, foot and body stones with heavy load beneath
Of fatal births and fevers and shipwreck-stricken grief.

Her voice is low, respectful with eternal fascination
Which attends the ends of others' lives, their final destination
She and Granny quietly muse upon the graveyard scene
Forget just for a moment their charge, the Lily queen.

They hear a plainsong voice, see her touch a stone
And make out she is reading as her mother's done
'I'm sorry you are dead and cannot see your friends
But when you're bad you all get killed and that is how it ends!'

Amazed they gazed at Lily
Stunned to silence, well almost
'Holy Mother' Granny said
Lily's mother, 'Holy Ghost!'

COMMONS TIME

I dreamed a dream of Torrington
Of forty years ago
Where we picnicked with the children
Sweet lullaby and low.

While the baby slept the afternoon
Her brothers fought a war
With sticks among the bracken
Black-bruised a grass-snake's lore.

Her sister gathered flowers
Speedwell and Celandine
And laid them by the infant
Oh communion cup divine.

Sheep safely grazed on Commons land
By rights this town affords
From bounteous liberality
Bestowed by ancient lords.

Echoes down the ages
Of Royalists' rendez-vous
Of fires, chance and intended
A warmth of déjà-vu.

Centuries of Commons
I dream then all as one
A thousand ages in their sight
Are like an evening gone.

DARK PASSAGE

The moon called in for coffee
Not here but down the road
That runs direct from my house
Towards the sun's abode.

He swung his dark cloak silently
And stunned the sun to night
She was desperate to be seen
As he blotted up her light.

She was used to common clouds
One has to be in Devon
Adored a clear blue sky
Her personal seventh heaven
But this was deep disturbing
And took away her breath
A sense of total snuffing
Of doom, impending death.

She shrank into a slim ellipse
Like meanest of new moon
But shot brief fiery glances
In red and dark maroon.

The earth was black as night
Birds puzzled made for roost
The dog slumped into bed
Thousands waited on the coast.

The moon may have had discomfort
From the sun's bright searing light
For he didn't linger long
When she gleamed out to the right.

Then it was all over
Earth was light as day
The sun smiled through the clouds
The moon had passed away.

Eclipse of the Sun; 11.8.99.   VJT

LIVES IN WAITING

Patience is the morning soft under the dew
Before the mists have rolled away and left a harsher view
Patience is an acorn in its textured cloak
Waiting long to start to grow and go for hearts of oak.

Patience is a baby waiting to be born
And the paining mother straining until the early dawn
Patience is the father waiting horny in the wings
While she gives affection rather to her newest king of kings.

Patience is the sister with the crying scrawny scrap
Suddenly she feels too old to fill her father's lap
Patience is the brother: how can you blow off steam
When your mother sits breastfeeding in front of your home team?

Patience is all parents, well those who don't resign
Waiting for their families to take them out to dine

Patience is a sick man letting doctors try
To cure with sickening treatments when he only wants to die
Patience is an oak tree standing broad for years
Spanning its last spring, spawning near its peers.

Patience is the dark yearning for the night
With relief beyond belief from the cruelty of light
Patience is the whole wide world through every revolution
Inexorably turning for Darwin's evolution.

PRIDE BEFORE THE FALL

You were loth to go
We knew you couldn't stay
Yet you lingered like that summer
Soft and gentle with each day.

Precious time stood still
Stolen nights together
Memories to last
For ever and for ever.

Somehow you took our daughter
Down the aisle as bride
She knew, you both walked tall
In triumph, joy and pride.

That dusk the swallows gathered
Wing by feather on the wire
And every eve for nigh two weeks
Waiting, circling ever higher.

You hung on, stretching summer
To the limit of your strength
Till the honeymoon was over
And you could go at length.

The leaving was so quiet
Full of hush and peace
Beautiful and painless
A truly rare release.

The wire was deserted
The birds had flown as well
And so this time of year
I feel compelled to tell
How with each September's swallows
I thankfully recall
Your chosen time of going
With pride before the Fall.

JONATHON

Jonathon you have grown up, but not grown out of your kind ways
Your shy sensitivity of boyhood yesterdays
I mind so well the New Years Eves when you and other revellers
Came back for food and cheer, a telling pair of levellers.

Come the morning you took time to help and talk to me
Not creeping, currying favour, just concerned maturity
So many years have passed, a quarter of life's span
I've seen you seldom, just enough to know a caring man.

Why else when newly widowed and in recovery hours
Would you contrive to quiet arrive with lovely golden flowers?

November '91

A few more years slip by, you ask me to your marriage
To Renata, girl of heart and soul: tall, elegant of carriage
A Catholic church, a smiling priest, warm-spirited relations
All thro the night reception: thanks, love, congratulations.

May '98

LOW FOOTING

I simply love high heels and as I'm rather short
(5' 3" in stocking feet) I've generally bought
Smart shoes that give me height, elevate my gaze
Into others' eyes and over broader ways.

I had quite a collection in every shade of leather
My favourite - French - in yellow, footlight as any feather
I was happy with my shoes, felt tall enough and neat
Two inches gave me confidence to stand on my own feet.

But - at a wedding in Slovakia, when we danced all thro' the night
And sang to local music and got a little tight
And discarded all the footwear amidst the stepping babel
And then the tights and stockings to footsie 'neath the table-

I suddenly felt pain under all my toes
Sharp, excruciating, oh nobody knows!
No longer could I dance at all, I sat and smiled, so brave
But in reality I felt like two feet in the grave.

And that was the beginning of my indisposition
A hampering of mobility, a mandatory submission
To ageing of important joints called osteoarthritis
Permanent, progressive, not fleeting like phlebitis.

So I had a consultation with the man who did my hip
Which I must say has been wonderful, enabled me to trip
To glorious foreign parts to climb and raft and camp
With no rusting or discomfort in spite of all the damp.

He was welcoming, concerned, said 'I did a good job there'
(Put my hip through all its paces) and fully I concur
However on the other, he had much less to say
You just cannot replace feet, maybe they will one day.

I had supports and tablets, he said 'See how it feels'
Frankly, not much better, - *and I can't wear my high heels!*
To resist the strong temptation, the best have left this home
For elder daughter Wendy, sadly something of a clone.

Footnote: Today I saw a young man who used to be a punk
　　　　　I said: 'My how you've grown,' but maybe it's me that's
　　　　　　　　　　　　　　　　　　　　　　　shrunk!

FLASHBACK

The guns were kept those days behind the kitchen door
In a specially-fashioned cabinet as is required by law
Strong-fastened to the wall with plugs and polyfilla
Inside the deadly weapons, one called a 'humane killer!'

Another crafted well, to some a joy to feel,
Left in a mentor's will, a man of fire and steel
They had been used in practice, perhaps at point-to-point
To kill a fallen horse with fracture near a joint -

- and for other livestock, tho' I get now the inflection
That many more are put to sleep with darts and soft injection
Sometimes awake at night, a wish would wax and wane
That thus my dying love could be relieved of pain.

His body barely cold, authority came knocking
To ask about the weapons and who would do the cocking
No I had no licence but couldn't this have waited
For a decent grieving interval, the papers be post-dated?

They grunted and they grumbled and growled, - the key was missing
Eventually agreed to go, soft murmuring and hissing
Later I took the case, illegally it's true
To my son, clone of his father, a sense of déjà-vu.

The space behind the door is painted, neat and clean
Like my single life to others, as if there'd never been
A guncupboard, a man to lend a sweet endeavour
The memories are proud and keen, the void is here for ever.

RED SKY AT NIGHT

A remembrance plaque now weathered
On a lichened stretch of wall
Above a marble table
Where passion flowers fall
Beneath a willow drop
A cream catkin cascade
Mixed with bland anemones
A Turkish carpet shade.

Welsh slate, grey, smooth-perfect
Holds a centaur at its dome
Emblem for the surgeon
Who was master of this home
Follows then his name
In letters bold and clear
He used to stand and view
The lake - and peace - from here.

Depicted at its base
With water waves and curly
Proud parent geese with goslings
Who island-nested early
One of the young swims eastwards
Alone against the tide
That was how my man survived
And lived until he died.

His ashes lie deep in the lake
Beneath the sunset fire
Which warms me, stirs me, drains me
Then lifts me gently higher
Here I find the comfort
To soothe my soul and start
To melt and move the memories
Relieve my bursting heart.

III   SEASONAL DELIGHTS

NEW BRIMSTONE, MOON AND PIPESTRELLE

Early March
Spring come too soon
With welcome warmth
Till well passed noon.

On silent hills
A light, a lift
From winter's tail.

First Brimstone flies
Down yellow vale
Of daffodils.

Like a flying petal
A floating note
From the flower's trumpet
Played sotto
Voce, skimming rills.

The moment flies
Is gone too soon
Cold evening sports
A brand new moon
And a Pipestrelle.

FRESH AIR

Each spring is better than the last
And takes me by surprise
When a soft wind blows its promise
Through pale blue cottoned skies
And shimmers blackthorn's leaf-bared blossom
Shafts primrose yellow light
Whispers dainty daffodils
To launch a Brimstone flight.

It stirs the long-grown winter lawns
And trees poised with buds on hold
Starlings waiting for their mating
Till sun warms grey to gold.

In the long drear of short winter days
When Christmas and family have been
I fear the mind's dark cloud may never lift
To let the spring come in
But the threshold of this changing season
Brings sharp anticipation
Of colour, light, revival
Re-birth a new gestation.

And each faithful spring is better than the last
And tho' I love the summer and the fall
I am truly convinced, today anyway
That my last spring will be the best of all.

MOONSHINE

Silver shafts of light
Palest of full moons tonight
Shifting through the trees.

Shimmers dance a tune
Halting suddenly too soon
As clouds ride the breeze.

A dark interlude
Hunters quietly rest and brood
Their prey take their ease.

Moonlight wins a glare
Lightens up a fox's lair
The scavenger's lees.

Moons will wax and wane
New to full then new again
Circling through the years.

Barn Owl. CRT

INDICTED

An owl sat staring
White as a gleam
Accusingly, piercing
From a dark beam.

A Barn Owl sat staring
My heart gave a leap
I'd missed her for years
The joy made me weep.

But her anger in staring
Defied all belief
Burned into my soul
My tears became grief.

I knew of her anger
For where could she go
When the old barn was flattened
And the building laid low?

I remembered my staring
In a winter of snows
As she dipped low at dusk
Along the hedgerows.

Downwards her staring
To make a decision
Zoom in on her prey
Cruel grace and precision.

Still she is staring
I know she well knows
Her hunting has gone
There are no hedgerows

Green intent plans
To put it all right
But by then she'll have taken
A much higher flight.

RECURRING THEME

This summer has been wet, more like a monsoon
Few garden teas or barbecues, so autumn comes too soon
The bog needs little doing, that garden's flourished well
All big-leaved wet and shady where Tawnies screech and yell
And this year's frogs have flopped about - happily they shimmer
In filtered light and so avoid my overactive strimmer.

Oh yes, it's 'mists and mellow fruitfulness' but there's end of
season clearing
Before the nights are all drawn in and thick frosts have a hearing
Which will sweeten all the parsnips: the peas and beans are finished
The Cabbage White has made quite sure the sprouts will be
diminished
Most of the lettuce bolted while I was away
But the onions are quite splendid and will last for many a day.

The courgettes were delicious picked when young and narrow
Yet every year there's one I miss until it's made a marrow
Beetroots are on the small side but well-rounded dark and neat
The peppers smooth and green, unconscionably sweet
I've emptied all the greenhouse, dug plants up with verve
Picked tail end green tomatoes for ritual preserve.

I've rooted all the cuttings of fuchsia and hydrangea
Hibiscus and geranium and one odd un-named stranger
Six purple aubergines on a single stalk
Firm slender cucumbers, good with pickled pork
The potatoes a disaster punished by the blight
Next year I'll move them on and use a virgin site.

Every year's the same but different and fresh
With the flowering and the fruitfulness from tended early crêche
Some say 'Oh all that work - refurbishing the pots
Forever cutting lawns, extending parsnip plots
You should move to somewhere smaller now you're not so young'
But I love this life's structure, I'll stay and dig the dung.

Green Goddess.   VJT

WORSHIPFUL IMAGE

She really is an icon
But so subtle, quiet and modest
It takes a second glance to know
The beautiful Green Goddess.

IV   WATCHING, WAITING AND WISHING

WINDOW-GLAZING

I'm sitting at the window
There's not a lot to see
The Fletcher's phlox is dying
And they're out at 33.

Oh but goodness, here's Miranda
With the newest baby boy
In a royal marine blue pram
Spick span and ship ahoy.

She looks prime pert and cocky
Turns her head to preen
Achieving life's endeavour
At just turned sweet sixteen.

She smiles at Ted the milkman
As he struggles with the key
(He's put old Winnie's milk inside
Since nineteen ninety three).

The dustman's due today
Maggie moved the sacks
To the gateless grey stone entrance
Full of gaping cracks.

I hope they come to time
Before the meals on wheels
Balanced by big Brenda
In her clip clop tip top heels.

Tomorrow will be Saturday
Sometimes the family calls
With all their searching questions -
'Have you had one of your falls?'

Well actually I have
But to tell would be my doom
I mean to stay and live my way
Here in my own front room.

THE NIGHTSHIRT

Nellie Dean stood waiting
Said sister 'Come with me
We'll go into the dayroom
And have a cup of tea.'

The day room housed some books
The pay phone and the tele
Nobody was there
Just anxious waiting Nellie.

Sister brought the steaming tea
With milk and sugar in
The cup had gilded flowers
And leaves around the rim.

'Mrs Dart, you know your husband
Had been ill for some time
This morning, well he changed
Up till then he seemed just fine.

He ate his toast for breakfast
Slowly washed and often sighed
Read the news and aired his views
And then . . . he quietly died.'

Mrs Dart was stunned
Flabbergasted, hurt
Her Fred was dead in bed
Without his fresh nightshirt.

She could not quite believe it
Last evening he'd been pert
She'd give the shirt to Maud
For her man, Fred's brother Bert.

THE FINAL STROKE

Norma's dead, after some weeks
Of drifting in a coma
Words gently failed to wake her
Nor soft touch nor sweet aroma.

She looked so perfect lying there
Nursed clean, tube fed and drained
With lingering pale suntan
Expression quite unpained.

Her eyes opened, wide staring
But did she comprehend?
Tempting to imagine not
But that's a dangerous trend.

One day I talked of everything
That recently I'd seen
Then bade farewell and squeezed her hand
She murmured 'Goodbye Jean!' . . .

What e'er befalls the body
Presume the mind is there
Its cells remain receptive
With resilience dead rare.

A VISION FOR THE FUTURE

If I could dream a future beginning here and now
I think I'd start with climate, so sunshine, - take a bow
Sun for garden teas on sleepy afternoons
Warm summer evening barbecues gliding through soft moons.

The weather makes our disposition
So often leaden skies
Drop rain and deep depression
Dark thoughts and heavy sighs.

It's hard to make decisions of optimistic mood
When all around is dreary (some compensate with food)
They say there's global warming proved by research that's been
                                                        done
But tho' the winter snows have gone, it's no fun without the sun.

I don't want sunshine all the time, that could perhaps be boring
Just enough to know it's summer, to give the season mooring
Then people might be brighter, more alert and more alive
Communicate more freely above depression's dive.

This tendancy could percolate
Through population's layers
The toddlers' group, the junior school
Teenagers doing highers
To their teachers and their parents
Thence their bosses and MPs
The happy mind of sunshine
Could colour all of these.

So . . .
More summer for the future
To give us all a boost
A milieu where calm reasoning
Can run and run, then roost.

V   REPAIRS!

ADMISSION

They put me in a side ward
With a red brick wall to view
And a window from the office
Not quite curtained through.

So the light shone on my eyes
When the ward was dark and dorm
I pulled up well the counterpane
And then got far too warm.

Nurse came in and plumped my pillows
I'd been on the brink of sleep
Counting weeping willows
And Devon Longwool sheep.

A girl groaned long, nurse called
The orthopaedic team
But later on I sunk into
A deep contented dream.

And then would you believe?
A sleeping pill prescribed
Was noisily presented
I woke and nearly cried!

They are all so attentive
I've not argued or denied it
But for what I'm looking for
I guess you must go private!

HERE AND NOW

This morning I know fear
I've got the hippy shake
My pulse is inter-city
My ache's become a quake

I've never been anaesthetised
No, not in my whole life!
Nor has any surgeon
Ever cut me with a knife.

Suppose it all goes wrong
And I lose my hippy leg
(I bet that's happened once)
And I end up with a peg.

Perhaps I'm hypersensitive
To that epidural
So I'll never walk again
Or see the world in plural.

I've waited for this treatment
Through many a painful bout
But now I look for reasons
To leave and chicken out.

The very worst to happen
Would be I'd wake up dead
The list is running late
Great, here comes the pre-med.

NIRVANA

Pills and pillows
Restless billows
Wills and will-o'-the-wisp
Strips and stains
Drips and drains
Whiteness done to a crisp.

Cleanliness
Light headedness
Copious analgesia
Distant pain
Felt again
After anaesthesia.

Life in limbo
Arms akimbo
Limp dependant tubes
Artificial
Sacrificial
Unsupported boobs.

I must wait
In this state
Entering the world
Trust my carers
Health repairers
Till my brain's unfurled.

PATIENT POSTURE

Arthritic pain has gone
But a dull confounded ache
Spreads down my leg and round my back
Hardly a piece of cake.

I wriggle this way and then that
To try and get some ease
Then sister spots my posture
'Uncross your legs now please!'

I uncross them right away
I've been told of this before
It's an automatic comfort
I've indulged for evermore.

I turn to lessen pressure
Use my good leg as a guide
And find blessed relief
Hear, 'Don't turn on your side!'

I try another pillow
Rotate to fix its place
'You must not turn about like that'
I nod with humble grace.

The physio said to move my toes
My ankles, knees and hips
She intended muscle tightening
Not full turnover flips.

So it seems I must lie straight
And stay upon my back
Possess my soul in patience
Something I know I lack.

They say it soon improves
With each long day that goes
I must attest now I can rest
And take a painless doze.

The dark drear nights are longest
The early tea sublime
One was longer than the rest
For British Summer Time!

DAWN CHORUS

'Wakey wakey half past six, drink your cup of tea
I'm going off duty now' night nurse says cheerily
'Wash your top half dear' - (another nurse has brought her
Trolley with a bowl of simply boiling water).

A flannel slop around, a towel pad and dab
Puff the magic talcum, spray the cologne fab
Now I am prepared to face the thin brown toast
With some sticky marmalade and the morning post.

Morning rush hour follows, staff skitter fore and back
Rose collects the tray, Maude the refuse sack
A buxom blond in blue plumps in with the hoover
Bangs around the beds, not a dainty mover.

Another comes in mauve with asthma and lordosis
(HRT when younger stays osteoporosis)
She's very gruff in countenance and voice too, says she'll spend
All her money on her smokes with none to leave or lend.

I favour the auxiliaries in their coffee check
Cheery, charming as they clear the ward's clinical deck
The routine chores are theirs, they get on and whistle through
All areas in their care, know what they must do.

The nurses 'better qualified'
Have more skilled jobs, to dress
The wounds, do drips and drains,
- less time to talk I guess.

MOVE!

The physio's here, get ready
Get up, get out of bed
Be bold, be brave, adventurous
And swing that leg of Pb.

She's short, she's white, she's agile
Her hair is cropped and chaste
Her hands are firm, supporting shoes
Black, sensible and laced.

Stand up straight, keep breathing
Place the crutches first
Bad leg, good leg, crutches
Try a second burst.

Proceed around the bed
Crutches, bad leg forward
That's good, good leg again
Then halfway down the ward.

Grim but grin and bear it
Turning can be tricky
Circle slow with little steps
Low bowling, wicket sticky.

Now for the homeward strait
The best bed is in sight
Exertion so exhausting
Gives dead sleep for the night.

EUPHORIA

They've done my hip replacement
And I'm still alive
That pain has gone already
I've walked up to Ward V!

GASTRIC GRUMBLES

Curry and rice today
But the rice looks more like maggots
And the heavily-spiced meat
Resembles ties of faggots
However I am hungry
And the flavouring quite good
Presentation not so vital here
As Floyd on 4 on food!

HIPPY HINTS

Make sure your nightie's not too fine
Remember you'll be taken
With halting steps right up the ward
Your muscles to awaken.

A faltering gait in later years
In full glare of the light
Showing bodyline through muslin
Is not a pretty sight.

Make sure your nightie's not too long
There danger lies in store
You need only to crutch one wrong
To sprawl across the floor.

Wear a gown with pockets
To walk recovery stage
To carry sweets, pens, dockets,
Hands otherwise engaged.

By all means look attractive
But it would be a pity
To forego practicalities
In order to look pretty!

HOME AGAIN, HOME AGAIN, CRUTCHETY CRUTCH

I've made it, I'm at home
My crutching's quite a feat
My hip is settling down
Like the top-up toilet seat.

At first the leg seemed long
(The one with the new hip)
Nurse said, 'That's an illusion
You've had a pelvic tip.'

Not a pleasant phrase
An unfortunate connotation
It worried me for days
But now the slant sensation
Has completely disappeared
So full marks to the nurse
Two legs of matching length
Are easier to reverse.

I've conquered all the stairs
Going down and up
My crutches come in useful
For controlling Tacker pup
Who has a taste for rubber
Bites wellies, chases tyres
And even rubber soles
Of trainers he admires.

Yet the crutches' rubber feet
Discourage his attention,
A chance to train her for a life
Of true rubber abstention.

CRUCIAL

Sticks insects ont l'habitude
Of thin uncovered limbs
They move with slow stability
And sip their summer Pimms.

Their bodies are in simple form
A set of jointed sticks
Straight bits deftly angled
A co-ordinated mix.

I love to watch their swinging gait
A slender pleasing pattern
I guess the insect musical
Could use one as a baton.

But my sticks are acquired
Just temporarily, I trust
Extensions aluminium of
My upper limbs, non - rust.

They are absolutely crucial
Give strong support, but light
For my hourly constitutional
Throughout the day and night.

I've learned to swing along
I keep my balance steady
Not as gainly as the insect
But success has made me heady.

VI   TOUCH OF TRAVEL

FLIGHT OF FANCY

We wait at Gate 63, Harare passengers and me
I look at the others, black fathers and mothers
With bright-eyed young kith and kin
They walk tall, they sparkle, make playful debacle
With white-toothed and open-wide grin.

Two lookalike men start walking again
They're tourists I'm certain like me
I think they're an item, talk ad infinitum
Their hand luggage fixed with a key.

Weathered white demands right: he's executive class
Exhibits his station with large corporation
Keeps distance from all the en masse.

Woman and man, unseasonal tan
With wrinkles and crinkles too soon,
After Christmas aplomb, they're making for home
And long afternoons in the sun.

White lady, old and shady
In broad-trimmed floppy hat - and chair
Darkly minder wheels behind her
Hung with gold earrings - and care.

So we wait at the Gate till 338 calls
And a flight in the sky to land by and by
In Zimbabwe, the home of the Falls.

Should the plain crash or land in a splash
Probably none would survive
Posh lady with perm, coloured, infirm
Executive, white, all dead in the night
Ah, we've landed, we're here
We're alive!

TRAPPED

Kariba
A lake made by man
Who stemmed the Zambezi
With a crossed nature dam.

Flooded
Dead trees stood leafless
Trunk tombs silver stark
Ghostly reminders
Which gleam after dark.

Shores
Currents, waves
Like treacherous seas
Subject to storms
Lightning drawn to the
trees.

Perches
For Kingfishers
Pied Malachite
Where clouds of Egrets
Roost for the night.

Beauty
Indeed
But at what cost?
The level is falling
Nature has lost.

Man
Has abused
The lake - sold its power
To more than intended
The water drops lower.

Kariba, - the lake made by man.   VJT

Nature
Produced
A five year drought
Unpredicted by man
The lake's drying out

Listen
Does anyone hear
The piercing screech
Of the Blacksmith's Plover
On the widening beach?

Sunsets
So glorious
Firing the lake
Disguising disaster
How long will it take?

Kariba
A lake made by man
Who stemmed the Zambezi
With a crossed nature dam.

VII   NEARER HOME

CHURCH FÊTE

Today St Michael's and All Angels holds its summer fête
With furling flags and competitions and cheap cream teas as bait
The sun shines bright and warm throughout this July day
For the morning preparations and the afternoon make hay.

The grass has all been manicured, quite short carpet-cropped
And trees with trailing branches, trimmed and lightly lopped
This is the vicarage garden's day for tho hardly flower-bordered
It must think 'someone cares to make me look so ordered.'

A woman of some substance gives the opening words
High up from the balcony with breathing space and birds
She is the new headmistress at our local secondary school
Earned respect already, some pupils think her 'cool'.

There's something here for everyone of any age and taste
They clamour for the home-made cakes with nigh indecent haste
Previous keepers of the books, secondhand but some look new
Frown flicker at the layout, but I see they've bought a few.

I carry a small camera as often is my wont
And take a sitting couple, they pose, she says 'Oh don't!'
At the crucial moment I hear a tell-tale zing
The film (on 39) is spent . . .I quickly change the thing
The vicar's wife espies me 'Could you do the photo stint?
We'll sell them in the Red Cross shop at 50p a print.'

So I advance with camera to study all the stalls
The new young bookstall vendors - bought songs from Music Halls
Bric-a-brac and draw with earnest ladies writing
A collection of fine prizes which makes it more exciting.

A farmer on the Skittles copes with the children's queue
A good scene for a photograph so I'm tempted to take two
The plants are quite impressive, neat potted, moist and labelled
Managed by our expert who's been a while disabled.

The organist does the hoop-la, mostly youthful players
Whose size dictates the distance, some really need a dais.

A novelty idea I hadn't come across
10p to hold a rabbit, guinea pig or mouse
The children seem to love this, cuddling with a gentle touch
As they do to see the dogshow, more interesting than Crufts.
They can ride a donkey, suddenly grow tall
See how they'll see as parents, looking down on all.

The optician as White Rabbit paints the children's faces
As if they've just flown in from other planets worlds and places
A smaller surface coloured in careful operation
By the vicar's daughter painting nails in hues of rare sensation.

Food is in abundance, fresh baking, the cream teas
A draw for lovely strawberry cakes, cold ice creams to please
In contrast to the barbecue - for hotter palates caters
Managed with experience on impressive apparatus.

All this and entertainment too, school children country dancing
To an instrumental small ensemble, really quite enchanting.

A day to remember, to store in memory's search
Lots of the people present are never seen in church
And yet they seem to need us for life's special dates
Like births, marriages and deaths and especially summer fêtes.

PS The sitting couple's picture (39th) - I had some doubt
(A pair of retired medics) - only 'oh don't' came out.

SATURDAY PUBTIME

Busy, buzzing, boozing, Saturday round noon
A harassed Mum requests, for Kylie a small spoon
She's in the family room with Kylie's sister Gail
While Dad props up the bar and knocks back fine real ale.

Fat cats in fancy hats are waiting for a wedding
Guarding gifts in plastic bags, glassware, bowls and bedding
Blue-rinsed ladies chatter in their usual places
Sometimes 'tutting' at the scene with gentlewomen's graces.

The cricket team is in 'preparing' for a match
Marvelling at last Sunday's game, the Captain's master catch
The girls behind the bar, dressed in cream and tall
Take cue from the manager who keeps his eye on all.

His voice is tinged with anger when weekenders park their van
To block the zimmer slope - 'how anybody can?'
Nobody calls time, they don't in pubs today
Hence drink is downed more slowly (?) in theory anyway.

The cricket team departs, weekenders move their van
The blue-rinsed ladies toddle home, Mum prizes out her man
Kylie and Gail have had enough, they're glad to be away
Skip down the zimmer slope to a sunny summer day.

Two old men have lingered
They love to hog the fire
Just like on every other day
To talk and sup and tire.

PADDINGTON STARE

I'm here rather early for my journey back to base
I drink indifferent coffee and observe the human race
As they criss-cross most with purpose, to start their programmed day
Not needing boomed announcements rolled inaudibly away.

Brief-cased businessmen, suggest substantial means
Amani specs, smart haircuts, one incongruously with jeans
A first class business woman, young, prematurely white
Floating long a sleeveless coat, skirt matching tailored tight.

A harassed lady traveller reads the board and sighs
Heavy bags in hand and more under her eyes
She finds the only seat and reluctantly it seems
Parks herself next to a tramp who sleeves his nose and beams.

Two young girls wolf burgers from the neighbouring bar
They bear enormous backpacks: how fine and fit they are.
They're also very beautiful and two young city clones
Glance sideways now and often around their mobile phones.

An excited group of children, destined may be for the Dome
Are herded by three adults: one has an itch to roam
Towards the smell of sausages and Daily Paper stack
His teacher spots him sidling off and pulls him smartly back -
Just in front of Moslem ladies three, elegantly covered
One with only eyes to see: with lowered gaze they hovered.

The table is updated, the board clicks on its way
It's time for me to go, back to Tiverton Parkway
Only two hours journey between two worlds apart
From pulsating Paddington to Devon's quiet heart.

VIII MUSIC

VELVET VOICES

The ladies of the Choral are a -Gondoliering
With a shortage of the menfolk and a keenness quite endearing
They've selected brand new dresses - whatever made them think
Of crushed strawberry velvet which, after all is pink?

Such a hue is difficult for anyone to wear
Unless she has complexion of blond or silver hair
Three or four are different, not pink - or mauve - or wine
But a shade that's hardly blending, way off the strawberry line.

They troop in with their copies, fresh-styled about the head
And take their proper places - oh dear! - the chairs are red!
The contraltos look quite musical, solid, deep and plump
Hardly fashion leaders, tho one wears a matching pump.

The sopranos are more varied in age, physique and shape
The heavy-bosomed leader is like a curtain drape
The pianist and conductor are hailed before they start
Also the turner-overer - it puts them in good heart.

The choruses come over well, the Gondoliers are bold
Contadine and Casilda are perhaps a little old
Gianetta's lost her voice, so there's a stand-in here
A blue sylph from Operatic with top notes sweet and clear.

In the theatre - cum - hall, cum-cinema, cum the rest
The ventilation's absent, but they sing on in full zest
The audience gets warm, never mind the choir
Whose frocks and faces glow in a melting strawberry fire
The habits are long-skirted, high-necked, tight-wrist, long-sleeved
Not by jewel, lace or trinket is the flush relieved.

We all enjoyed ourselves, sincerely this is stated
Their offering musicale should not be underrated
But as the audience left (they praised the choir I stress)
There were some criticisms of the brand new velvet dress
One lady from another choir said 'my dear what a sight!'
Most agreed and I concede, you can't beat black and white.

- like the menfolk

VON HIMMEL HOCH
(From Heaven Above)

I rarely dream - but I hear music
At strange and stirring times
Something I remember
Like childhood nursery rhymes
A familiar rhythm linking
With precision rare and daunting
Time waves of deep emotion
Warm, comforting, yet haunting.

It commenced when I was very young
Too young to know of Bach
Yet in retrospect it seems
It's always had that master's mark
Is it just imagination
That this is ever how it's been?
An air that now I recognise
As Von Himmel hoch, a Christmas theme.

This melody is mine
Played by a soothing muse
A gentle, supporting, - yet
Sometimes disturbing ruse
But since it's been identified
And I've half mastered its playing
With hands and organ feet
The music's been quite absent, staying
Out of earshot
For nigh on seven years
Lingering only in the memory
Of laughter, love and tears.

May be if I reach the pearly gates
Von Himmel hoch will thunder - and
While Bach stands there and smiles
Will rent with joy my soul asunder.

IX   JUBILEE

GOD SAVE THE QUEEN

A Golden Jubilee Celebration for the Queen
Is it really fifty years since I remember having been
At her coronation?
With Mum and Dad and sister Anne along the Mall we stood
In crushing milling throngs for the sight of royal blood
In joyous expectation.

People laughed and shouted, the waiting crowd bemused
By wandering child, lone cyclist. They passed the time, amused
Through long anticipation
Policemen started grouping, music positive and clearer
Beat excitement with the heart, brought the procession nearer
The hush of veneration.

Then 'she's here' they cried aloud, and eventually she came
In carriage closed for with her came the English rain
We opened the umbrella
It was just a glimpse but memory keeps the sparkle
Of her jewels and dress of course but also her young smile's mark'll
Stay with me for ever.

(The charismatic Queen of Tonga, older, well-endowed
Lay back in open carriage, waved flamboyantly for the crowd
Elle avait l'habitude)

So half a century on, she and I are still around
Survived families' entourage since she was Abbey crowned
And set a royal mood
She's not a slave to fashion of culture, whim or clothes
But has refreshing constancy, so comforting to those
Who fear aberration.

She seemed surprised by crowds so supportive - and their size
Some of us surprised ourselves and wondered, was it wise
To prepare these celebrations?
But oh in retrospect, it really was worthwhile
The tea, the flags, the fancy dress with all the rank and file
In participation
Long live the Queen, thanks for her continuity
May the faith which she has kept pass on in perpetuity
For this privileged population.